IMAGES
of America

DETROIT
1860–1899

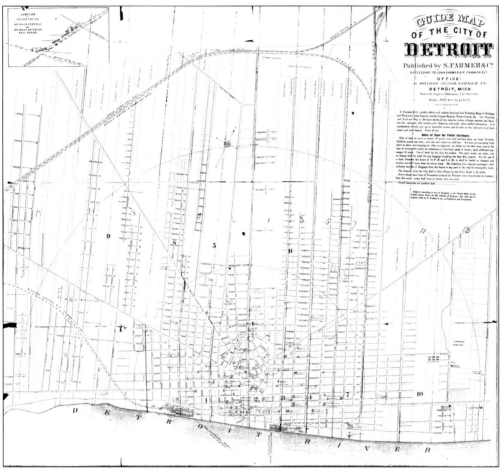

A Street Map of the Heart of Detroit, 1861. This map helps place the photographs shown here in their proper perspectives.

IMAGES
of America

DETROIT
1860–1899

David Lee Poremba

ARCADIA

Published by Arcadia Publishing,
an imprint of Tempus Publishing, Inc.
2 Cumberland Street
Charleston, SC 29401

Printed in Great Britain.

Library of Congress Catalog Card Number: 98-85884

For all general information contact Arcadia Publishing at:
Telephone 843-853-2070
Fax 843-853-0044
E-Mail arcadia@charleston.net

For customer service and orders:
Toll-Free 1-888-313-BOOK

Visit us on the internet at http://www.arcadiaimages.com

To my grandchildren, Amanda, Andrew, Kyle, Ian, and Samantha.
And for Kate.

Contents

Acknowledgments

To all the archivists and librarians of the Burton Historical Collection, past and present, whose careers have been dedicated to preserving and sharing the past. All photographs shown in this work are here courtesy of the Burton Historical Collection of the Detroit Public Library.

Introduction

Detroit, the city of the straits, was founded on July 24, 1701, by a group of 100 French and Indian explorers led by a man named Antoine de la Mothe Cadillac. The small fort they built was ideally situated on a tall bluff overlooking the narrowest section of the river. They would be able to control the fur trade of the old Northwest, coming form the upper to the lower Great Lakes. It would be that way for the next 140 years, under the flags of three different countries (France, Great Britain, and the United States), until the furs lost their value. Then the city's geographic situation would again serve to give her easy access to raw materials from the forest, soil, and mines and make Detroit a great manufacturing city.

By 1860, Detroit had grown to become a bustling community of some 45,000 people, the nineteenth largest city in the United States. They were a diverse group of people—ethnic, cultural, and economic backgrounds differed greatly. They were of African, Native American, German, French, English, Polish, and Dutch descent, and they lived and worked together to make Detroit the leading city of the Midwest. Detroit's economic diversity helped make it a pioneer in the West in iron manufacture, converting iron ore into pig iron. It was a leader in the production of Bessemer Steel, and in the rolling of steel rails. Detroit was the largest manufacturer of freight cars for the railroad and was the original home of the Pullman sleeper. The city was also the second largest producer of pharmaceuticals, second only to New York. Detroit took the lead from New York in the stove-making industry, producing cooking stoves and ranges, heating stoves, gas ranges, and electric heaters and furnaces. The city was also among the leaders in the paint and varnish industry, as well as a leading producer of plant, flower, and fruit seeds. Detroit led the way in ship building in the Great Lakes along with the manufacture of ornamental and useful hardwoods. This industrious city even used the salt beneath the streets to lead the way in the production of alkalis and other salts.

During the years illustrated here, 1860–1899, Detroit grew from a frontier town to one of the greatest manufacturing cities of the nineteenth century. The following photos offer a glimpse of that growth, as well as a look at how and where Detroiters lived, worked, and played. We are able to watch as the city expands, greatly overshadowing, but never forgetting, the tiny fort on the bluff.

One

The 1860s

CHRISTIAN HENRY BUHL—MAYOR OF DETROIT 1860–1862. Born in Pennsylvania in 1812, he came to Detroit in 1833 and, together with his brother Frederick, built up a profitable hat and fur business. In 1855 Christian formed the wholesale hardware house of Buhl & Ducharme and helped develop Michigan's steel, mining, and railroad industries. He died in 1894.

BIRD'S-EYE VIEW OF THE CITY OF DETROIT IN 1860. From a wood engraving, this view shows the bustling riverfront and the Michigan Central Railroad roundhouse where train engines were rotated onto different tracks. In the distance one can count at least seven church steeples. Detroit had a population of 45,619 people in 1860.

MICHIGAN CENTRAL RAILROAD PASSENGER DEPOT. This terminal was located at Third and Woodbridge Streets and served its customers from 1835 until it was destroyed by fire in 1912. The billboard advertisement right next door directs passengers to the terminals of the Grand Trunk Railroad of Canada. A freight wagon and horse-drawn omnibus await their cargoes. In the background is the Cass Hotel, and an excellent example of a gas streetlight is in the foreground.

STOCKHOLDERS

OF THE UNDERGROUND

R. R. COMPANY

Hold on to Your Stock!!

The market has an upward tendency. By the express train which arrived this morning at 3 o'clock, fifteen thousand dollars worth of human merchandise, consisting of twenty-nine able-bodied men and women, fresh and sound, from the Carolina and Kentucky plantations, have arrived safe at the depot on the other side, where all our sympathising colonization friends may have an opportunity of expressing their sympathy by bringing forward donations of ploughs, &c., farming utensils, pick axes and hoes, and not old clothes; as these emigrants all can till the soil. N. B.—Stockholders don't forget, the meeting to-day at 2 o'clock at the ferry on the Canada side. All persons desiring to take stock in this prosperous company, be sure to be on hand.

Detroit, April 19, 1853.

By Order of the
BOARD OF DIRECTORS.

UNDERGROUND RAILROAD. Broadsides such as these were placed around the city notifying freedom-loving people of the safe arrival in Canada of 29 fugitive slaves from the Carolina and Kentucky plantations. Detroit was one of the northern "terminals" on the Underground Railroad with at least one station on the line.

FINNEY BARN. At the northeast corner of Griswold and State Streets stood the Finney barn, one of the stations on the Underground Railroad. Still a stable in this later photograph, the barn was a place of refuge for escaped slaves before they finally crossed the river into Canada and freedom.

FEDERAL POST OFFICE, APRIL 20, 1861. When President Lincoln's call for troops to defend the Union arrived in Michigan, these able-bodied citizens gathered at the corner of Larned and Griswold Streets to hear patriotic speeches and to take the oath of allegiance. Spectators gathered on rooftops to see and hear the proceedings. James Roys's bookstore and news depot had its largest crowd, while the Capitol Union High School stood alone at the end of Griswold Street.

FORT WAYNE, APRIL 1861. Men of the First Michigan Volunteer Infantry (enlisted for three months) take a break from training at the portcullis of the fort. Formed from the various private militia companies from Detroit, Jackson, Coldwater, and other outlying communities, this unit would be ready to depart for Washington within the month.

CAMPUS MARTIUS, MAY 11, 1861. The men of the First Michigan marched from Fort Wayne to Campus Martius opposite city hall for this special public ceremony. Thousands of citizens watched as the Ladies of Detroit presented the colors to the regiment. Speeches were given by prominent Detroiters such as Henry A. Morrow, George Duffield, and the unit's commanding officer, Colonel Orlando B. Willcox, before marching to the docks and returning by boat to Fort Wayne. Two days later, the men departed for the front. Shortly after their arrival in Washington, the first western regiment to reach the capitol, they were addressed by the President, who is said to have greeted them with, "Thank God for Michigan." They fought courageously at the first Battle of Bull Run, losing 117 of their 500 officers and men, including their commander, who was shot off his horse and captured. The spire of the First Presbyterian Church dominates the scene and the diversity of businesses can be viewed along Woodward and Monroe Avenues. Ling and Chandler manufactured melodeons, which were small reed organs.

FORT WAYNE, SUMMER 1861. These men of the Second Michigan Infantry go through their drill at the fort. Over the course of the conflict, the State of Michigan contributed almost 90,000 men to the Union army, over 85,000 of them volunteers. This regiment was also made up of militia companies and was enlisted for three years—the first Michigan unit to be recruited as such.

FORT WAYNE, SUMMER 1861. The officers of the Second Michigan Volunteer Infantry pose for a formal portrait along officer's row at the fort. Israel B. Richardson of Pontiac was the commanding officer, and Henry L. Chipman, the second in command. The regiment fought in both the eastern and western theaters of war.

BRUSH STREET, AUGUST 1861. The First Michigan Regiment returns to Detroit after serving its three-month commitment. The men are greeted by the enthusiastic citizens of Detroit at the Brush Street station of the Detroit and Milwaukee Railroad. Judge Charles Irish Walker delivered the welcoming address and, following the parade of the veterans, the Ladies of Detroit gave the returning heroes a splendid banquet.

BRUSH STREET, 1861. The Detroit and Milwaukee Railroad boasted of fares that were $3 less than any other route and provided a "cheap, pleasant, and expeditious route." The line had two express trains leaving Detroit for Pontiac, Holly, Fentonville, Flint, Saginaw, and all points on the Mississippi River.

KINCHEN ARTIS. The only known photograph of an enlisted man in uniform of the First Michigan Colored Infantry, Corporal Artis is a fine example of the over 1,000 African Americans who served in the Union ranks from Michigan. He enlisted at Battle Creek in 1863 for a term of three years, and was mustered out at Charleston, South Carolina, in September 1865. After the war he lived in Detroit and later settled in Romeo, where he died in 1905.

WOODWARD AND CONGRESS, 1862. Looking south toward Jefferson, one can see the triumphal arch erected to celebrate the safe return of Brigadier General Orlando B. Willcox from Confederate captivity at the infamous Libby Prison. The emergence of Woodward Avenue as the main artery of the city is evidenced by the number of different businesses present. The one-horsepower trolley and the lone rider are examples of the sole methods of transportation. Hitching posts line both sides of the street.

WOODWARD AND JEFFERSON, 1860s. This close-up view of a busy intersection shows various types of carriages and buggies. On the left is the J.W. Frisbie & Company dry goods store at 167 Jefferson, alongside Martin S. Smith's jewelry. Another dry goods store and the Aetna Life Insurance Company are in the 60th block of Woodward.

CAPITOL UNION HIGH SCHOOL, 1865. This building served as the State's first capitol on Griswold Street when Detroit was the territorial capitol—hence the name for the high school. Henry Chaney was the principal, and the top floor was occupied by the 5,200 volumes of the Detroit Public Library.

RUSSELL HOUSE, 1865. Located on Woodward near Campus Martius, this popular hotel was built in 1836 and rebuilt in 1882 before being razed in 1905. It was formerly known as the National Hotel. Behind the hotel can be seen the twin spires of Saint Anne's Church, which was located on the north side of Larned between Bates and Randolph.

JEFFERSON AVENUE, 1860S. This view, looking eastward toward Waterworks Park, shows the Biddle House (right), another of the city's popular hotels. Augustus Taber was the Biddle's proprietor, who also wholesaled liquors, wine, and tea. The First Congregational Church is to the left in the photo, while the tower of the Waterworks at Orleans Street can be seen in the distance.

HARPER HOSPITAL, 1865. On Woodward Avenue near Fremont, Harper Hospital was founded on May 4, 1863. During the Civil War it served as a United States Military Hospital. The Reverend George Duffield served as its president. Mr. Walter Harper deeded the land which was outside the city limits, beyond the "Farm Line." Mrs. Nancy Martin, a grocer, also deeded some acres at Martin Place and Woodward.

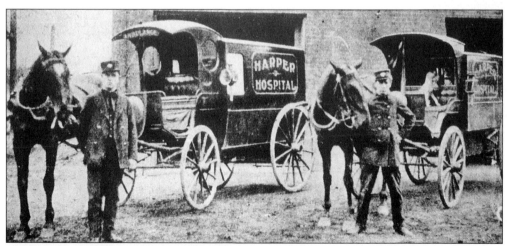

HARPER HOSPITAL AMBULANCES. These horse-drawn ambulances provided emergency services to Detroiters when the hospital was opened for service to the general public on January 1, 1866. The first sessions of the Detroit College of Medicine would take place three years later.

WAYNE STREET, JUST NORTH OF LARNED. Here is a typical example of the fire stations of the Civil War period. This engine house and its watchtower were built in 1857. The construction of taller buildings and the invention of the telephone ended the usefulness of these watchtowers by the 1880s.

FIREMAN'S HALL, 1860S. Located at the corner of Larned and Bates Streets, Fireman's Hall served as a meeting place for different groups and was also an excellent location for concerts.

GRISWOLD AND WOODBRIDGE STREETS, 1860S. One of Michigan's oldest continuous newspapers, the *Detroit Free Press*, moved to this building on the northwest corner of Griswold and Woodbridge Streets in the fall of 1859. The *Daily Free Press* was published every morning and evening; it cost 25¢ per week or $10 per year.

SHELBY AND LARNED STREETS, 1867. The staff of the *Detroit Daily Post* take time out of their busy day to be photographed in front of their new quarters. Saint Paul's Episcopal Church, at the corner of Shelby and Congress, can be seen at the extreme left.

EAST JEFFERSON AVENUE, 1867. This photograph of an original painting by Frederick E. Cohen depicts the Joseph Campau house in the 140 block of Jefferson, east of Woodward. This house was built in 1813 and survived the growth of the garment district around it until it was demolished in 1880.

LARNED STREET, BETWEEN FIRST AND SECOND STREETS. According to legend, this house was built at the river for a Huron chief at the command of Cadillac in 1703. More likely built in the 1740s, this home was occupied by Lewis Cass and was known as the White House of the Northwest, after his appointment as territorial governor. James Monroe, the first president to visit Detroit, stayed here.

FORT STREET, 1860s. These young ladies appear to be dressed in their Sunday best on this cheery morning in springtime, in what looks to be an elegant neighborhood. In the far distance is the spire of one of Fort Street's glorious churches.

FORT STREET AND CASS AVENUE, 1860s. Built in 1840, this house was one of the last owned by Lewis Cass. It was situated on the northwest corner of Fort and Cass on the huge parcel of land known as the Cass farm. It is an excellent example of the architectural style of the period. It was removed in 1876.

FORT AND SECOND STREETS, 1860S. The residence of Senator Zachariah Chandler sat on the northwest corner of Fort and Second. Chandler was Detroit's first millionaire, a dry goods merchant, land owner, and a founder of the Republican Party. He served as a United States senator from Michigan during the Civil War and was a leader in the Underground Railroad at Detroit.

CAMPUS MARTIUS, APRIL 1865. Detroiters gather in the square to hear the news of the assassination of President Abraham Lincoln. As in any frontier town, the public square was the place to disseminate information quickly to the most people. Marcus Stevens's furniture store, Andrews's Railroad Hotel, and the new Odd Fellows Hall occupy the scene.

CAMPUS MARTIUS, APRIL 1865. The United States flags flying at half-staff in this photo indicate that this is a memorial to the slain president. This shot was taken from the south looking north. Henry Weber's furniture store is on the extreme right, next to the Boston Shoe Store. Blake & Seeley are partners in another furniture store. Notice the abundance of umbrellas.

GRISWOLD AND MICHIGAN AVENUES, 1866. The building at the extreme left is the city hall, built in 1835 and torn down in 1872. The building on the right is the Detroit Female Seminary, an all-girls school which gave the ladies a chance for an education. One hundred pupils were enrolled there.

CAMPUS MARTIUS, EAST SIDE, JULY 4, 1866. The citizens of Detroit gather to celebrate Independence Day with a parade, even though public buildings, such as the city hall (shown here), are still draped in mourning for President Lincoln. They are assembled here at the seat of city government to hear patriotic speeches given by prominent citizens and politicians.

WOODWARD AVENUE, JULY 4, 1866. This is a close-up of the parade as it moves down Woodward toward the river. It is a good example of the types of themes prevalent in American life, as in the Independence Day (1776) "float" in the middle of the photograph.

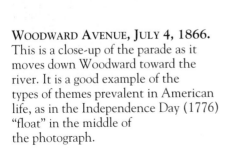

WOODWARD AVENUE, JULY 4, 1866. This long shot looking south along the parade route shows the extent of the crowds that gathered. In the background can be seen the temporary triumphal arch erected across Woodward at Jefferson Avenue.

CAMPUS MARTIUS, JULY 4, 1866. This close-up shows one of the "floats" of the parade—a replica ship from Detroit's Revolutionary War days, or perhaps a ship signifying Perry's victory on Lake Erie. The building behind the tree at right is the city hall.

WOODWARD AVENUE, EAST SIDE, 1867. In this view looking north, the development of Woodward as the main artery of the city is evident by the number of different businesses along it. These stores range from clothing, carpeting, dry goods, groceries, hardware, and a pharmacy. Delivery carts are evident, along with a number of customers.

WOODWARD AVENUE AT STATE STREET, 1869. The different architectural styles are displayed here, as well as the various uses of these buildings. The Martin S. Smith jewelry company moved to the top floor from its earlier location and shared space with a job printer and St. Andrews Bazaar. The city is still lit by gas.

CATHERINE STREET, 1860S. At number 57 Catherine Street, Bernard Stroh started his brewery business. There were over 25 different brewers in the city dotting the predominately German east side. It was definitely a family business, complete with children and pets, and was operated out of his home.

BATES STREET, 1869. Looking north along Bates Street, which ran from the river to Farmer Street, one can see a typical near-east-side neighborhood. William Archenbronn's tailor shop, William Wade's blacksmith shop, John Schuetz's beer hall, a billiards hall, and a boarding house make up this block. The church spire on the right is the Scotch Presbyterian Church.

CAMPUS MARTIUS, EAST SIDE, 1869. The number of wagons parked in front of the city hall illustrates the main source of transportation to the city center and suggests an important meeting in progress inside. John Copeland & Company's Palace Bakery was in a prime location, serving both city officials and the Russell House next door. The city streets are paved with cobblestones, and tracks for horse-drawn trolleys run down the middle.

TWO OX-POWER TRANSPORTATION. On a visit to the city, these suburbanites pose for a photo on a city street. Work-day fashions abound and teamwork is displayed as the man holds the reins and the woman operates the brake.

MICHIGAN AVENUE TROLLEY. Opened for traffic in November 1863, this line operated 3 track miles along Michigan Avenue to Thompson Street (Twelfth Street). These cars were 16 feet long and had no heat. Straw was laid down on the floor to keep passengers' feet warm.

GRATIOT AVENUE TROLLEY. Opened for traffic in September 1863, the Gratiot line operated from downtown to Russell Street, about 2 miles long. The cars were first built in Troy, New York, and originally remained on the tracks after they were finished with the days work. Later, a car barn was built to store them behind the Cass Hotel on Third Street. The fare was 5¢.

FREE GROCERY DELIVERY. As most workers were occupied with their jobs for 10 to 12 hours per day, there was little time to complete household chores. J.W. Lawhill offered free delivery of his wares throughout the city's neighborhoods.

EARLY MORNING MILK RUN. The milkman stops for a photograph with his dog while on his early morning rounds. A good example of mid-nineteenth-century home architecture is seen in the background. Homes such as this grew up side-by-side with neighborhood businesses.

WINTER TRANSPORTATION. This snappy one-horse, two-seater sleigh enabled Detroiters to travel from place to place during the winter months. These gentlemen on Woodward Avenue appear to be on their way to the office.

THIRD STREET, 1860S. One form of winter recreation was ice skating. This large lot along Third Street provided plenty of room for couples to enjoy themselves. Note the rather formal attire worn by the couple in the foreground.

CAMPUS MARTIUS, 1868. Plans were developed for a new, larger city hall, and this photograph depicts the laying of the cornerstone of that building. As is evident from the crowd, it was quite an event with bunting and flags flying. The Masonic fraternity laid the cornerstone with all due ceremony. Tickets had to be purchased to witness the event, attend the banquet, and sit in a carriage to view the parade. The parade involved no less than seven bands, city militia units, and the Fourth United States Artillery Battery from nearby Fort Wayne. The new city hall would be completed in three years.

Two

The 1870s

ALEXANDER LEWIS—MAYOR OF DETROIT 1876–1877. Alexander Lewis was born in Sandwich, Ontario, in 1822. Lewis came to Detroit in 1837, where he worked in a general store for $4 a month. In 1842 he formed his own freight-forwarding and commission company, and by 1862 he opened a flour and grain business, from which he gained a considerable fortune and was able to retire in 1884. He owned a substantial amount of downtown property and served as a director for several important financial institutions in the city. Lewis was president of the Detroit Gas Company. He and his wife, Elizabeth, had 13 children, 8 of whom lived to adulthood. Lewis ran for, and was elected, mayor on a law-and-order platform in 1876, following a two-term Republican. He governed a city of 101,225 souls.

Jefferson Avenue and Randolph, 1870. In a typical business day, some wares were moved to the curbside for sale or transportation. A new Fireman's Hall is squeezed in between a wine merchant and a liquor dealer. Oscar Hesselbacher was a confectioner and caterer who lived above his business in the 200 block of Jefferson.

Griswold Street, 1870s. This was known as the Seitz Block, after the bankers, Frederich L. and John H. Seitz, whose bank was at 53 Griswold. The building in the middle of the photo is the Goldsmith, Bryant, & Stratton Business University. William Jennison had a law office above the cigar store.

WOODWARD AND JEFFERSON AVENUES, 1870. Looking south toward the river, one can see the profusion of trolley tracks heading in several directions along both streets. Kings Clothing was located at 174 Jefferson Avenue and shared space with Messieurs Chappell and Van Duzen, agents for the Howe Sewing Machine Company.

JEFFERSON AND WOODWARD AVENUES, 1870, LOOKING WEST. Mr. A.C. McGraw owned the boot and shoe wholesale business at 69 Woodward Avenue. As we look down West Jefferson, there are mostly clothing and furniture wholesalers and retailers in this burgeoning business district. Is anyone else curious about this horse and wagon left alone in the middle of the intersection?

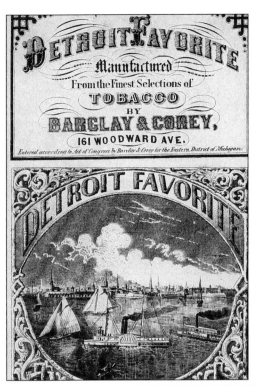

Detroit Favorite, 1870. Although listed in the City Directory only once, this advertisement piece illustrates the diversity of manufacturing in Detroit. The tobacco and cigar industry boasted at least three cigar manufacturers and a dozen tobacconists. The artist's illustration shows a busy Detroit River with both commerce and pleasure craft.

Woodward and Michigan Avenues, 1871. This is part of the crowd that was witnessing the opening of the new city hall on July 4, 1871. The Weber Company Warerooms boasted every kind of furniture, including billiard tables and pianos. The daguerrean gallery near the corner must have done a banner business in tintypes and other portraits.

38

FROM THE OLD TO THE NEW CITY HALL, JULY 4, 1871. The Detroit Common Council is seen here moving from the old city hall to the new one across the street. Henry Starkey and George W. Balch lead the procession of aldermen from the ten voting wards of the city. Here is a venerable array of top hats and whiskers. Note the lone police escort.

MICHIGAN AVENUE, 1872. Looking east to the Market Building, this view shows both city halls and best represents the exploding growth of Detroit. The old city hall would be torn down by the end of the year. The Great Western Hoop Company, with hoop frames hanging in the front of the store, is at the extreme right.

CITY HALL, 1870s. The majesty of the center of Detroit's government is evident in this photograph taken after the building is completed and the block landscaped. The clock has been installed in the tower and the four statues, which depict LaSalle, Cadillac, Father Marquette, and Gabriel Richard, are in place.

MARKET STREET, 1870s. These two gentlemen are part of the atmosphere surrounding the central market area of the city. They could be members of the Lime Kiln Club, a group of expert white-washers, who waited patiently for jobs to come to them. The more successful of them owned handcarts, while the lesser carried the tools of their craft in a bucket.

CAMPUS MARTIUS, APRIL 9, 1872. Over 25,000 people crowded into the city at the beginning of April to witness the unveiling of the Soldiers and Sailors Monument in front of the old city hall on Campus Martius. First conceived in 1861, this monument honors the Michigan soldiers and sailors who fought in the Civil War. The sculpture was commissioned in 1867 and unveiled on the anniversary of the end of the war.

CAMPUS MARTIUS, APRIL 9, 1872. A thunderous cheer goes up as the flags are drawn clear and the monument is unveiled. The citizens of Detroit raised $75,000 for this work of art. No less than 14 general officers were present, and Generals Burnside, Sheridan, and Custer gave speeches. Chief Parade Marshall General Alpheus Williams oversaw the huge parade down Woodward Avenue.

PARADE CLEAN-UP. These members of the Department of Public Works pause from their labors in keeping the city streets clean for a photograph. With Detroit's penchant for having a parade at the drop of a hat, their's must have been a full-time job.

WOODWARD AVENUE AND CAMPUS MARTIUS, 1872. The hustle and bustle of the era is evident as these ladies "hustle" their "bustle" to make the Grand River trolley connection. The building behind the trolley is the firm of Wright, Kay & Company jewelers, founded originally by R.J.F. Roehm in 1861.

CAMPUS MARTIUS, 1872. This is one last look at the building that served as the city's seat of government since 1835. After several attempts to find businesses or groups to occupy the structure, city officials opted to have it torn down. Note the Soldiers and Sailors Monument is without its second-tier statues.

WOODWARD AVENUE, NORTH OF GRAND RIVER, 1874. Known as the Barnes Block, this strip of retail outlets proudly displays their wares at curbside to anyone who happened to walk by. A variety of goods and services could be had here and, if you were tired, you could avail yourself of the wares at the curb.

JOSEPH CAMPAU AT THE RIVER, 1875. Doctor Samuel P. Duffield found a willing business partner in Hervey C. Parke, and they built their brick factory on Joseph Campau Street. Along with George S. Davis, a wholesale drug salesman, they began to manufacture pharmaceuticals in standardized drug strengths. In two years they were making a profit.

PARKE-DAVIS AND COMPANY, 1877. These ladies are hard at work preparing vaccines. The Parke-Davis Company financed several expeditions to Mexico, the West Indies, and the Fiji Islands to search for new medicinal plants and was among the first to understand the usefulness of animal glands in making medicines.

LARNED AND GRISWOLD STREETS, 1870S. The building on the left is the Federal Post Office, built in 1860. The city had 20 postal districts. The free delivery system was a success, and there was one collection in business districts made on Sunday afternoons. The Atlantic and Pacific Telegraph Company had an office at 39 Woodward Avenue. At this time, the city is beginning to get wired.

BATES AND CONGRESS STREETS, LOOKING NORTH FROM CONGRESS, 1875. This short block ran north into the central market area, and soon after this photograph was taken much of it was torn down and replaced by a number of three- and four-story hotels.

WOODWARD AND FORT STREET, 1874–75. Known as the Hog Block, this stretch of businesses offered a variety of goods for both city and suburban dwellers. Teas, candies, foreign fruits, the ever-present clothing and shoe outlets—even agricultural implements, whips, and lashes—could be had here. There was even a novelty clothing house.

WOODWARD AVENUE, 1870S. This block of Woodward clearly illustrates the variety of goods that were available to the consumer. It also reflects the character of the business owners, as the Fishers, Bakers, Wamsleys, Fords, and Welz's competed in a good-natured manner.

46

CADILLAC SQUARE, 1875. The Central Market, opened in the 1840s, was a place for produce growers, livestock dealers, harness makers, and farmers to sell and trade their products to city dwellers in an open-air market place. Originally only vegetables and meats were exhibited, but later almost anything, except lodging, might be bargained for.

CENTRAL MARKET, 1870s. Saturday was market day in Detroit and the variety of fresh produce is seen here. Confectionery, fruits, shoes, poultry, stockings, laces, meats, and fish could also be purchased or bargained for at the Central, or City Hall, Market. Labor could also be purchased—wood sawyers being found on the west end, and white washers and day laborers on the east end.

WOODWARD AND MICHIGAN AVENUES, 1875. The growing prosperity of the city can be seen in this photo of what was referred to as "the Majestic Corner." Many of the more elegant places to shop, eat, and recreate could be found around this thriving intersection. Note the street repair and movement of the carriages.

WOODWARD AVENUE BETWEEN STATE STREET AND GRAND RIVER, 1876. The west side of Woodward looking north shows a profusion of fancy goods establishments, starting on the extreme left with Kate and Sarah Brennan's hair salon and continuing with a wig maker, three booksellers, Butterick Patterns, and Mrs. H. Foex's fancy goods shop. The shoemaker in the foreground made boots for many of these smart business owners.

WOODWARD AVENUE BETWEEN GRAND RIVER AND CLIFFORD STREET, 1876. The west side of Woodward shows some of the older types of business/living quarters that were soon to be replaced with bigger, better buildings. The building on the extreme right was James Vernor's drugstore, where he sold a concoction called ginger ale.

JAMES VERNOR, 1870S. The first registered pharmacist in Michigan, James Vernor returned to Detroit after extensive service in the Civil War and opened his drugstore on Woodward Avenue. He discovered a good formula for making ginger ale and installed a soda fountain for over-the-counter sales. Receipts jumped dramatically, and he soon devoted all of his time to the making of ginger ale.

MONROE AND CONGRESS STREETS, 1870s. Baries Hat and Cap Factory was at 16 East Congress, in the first block east of Woodward. A good many of the city's streets are still dirt roads, and the wooden sidewalks can be seen in this photograph. The small portable structure in the center is a photographer's studio.

WOODWARD AVENUE AND CAMPUS MARTIUS, 1878. In a scene looking toward the northeast, the new Detroit Opera House is at the right of the picture. The church spire dominating the center belongs to the First Presbyterian Church. The white building to the church's left at 160 Woodward is Finney's Hotel, whose barn was a station on the Underground Railroad.

50

FORT STREET, LOOKING WEST FROM WAYNE STREET TOWARD WOODWARD AVENUE, 1870S. As this wagon heads toward the Central Market, we can see the Hiram Walker home and C.J. Whitney's music store. The building in the middle, in the distance, is the new city hall.

FORT STREET, LOOKING WEST TOWARD THE CITY LIMITS, 1877. Whitney's Music Store was at 40 West Fort Street and can be seen in this rare aerial view of the near west side. The mixture of residences and businesses can be seen, as well as three church spires, which are the First Congregational at Fort and Wayne, Grace Episcopal at Second, and the Fort Street Presbyterian Church at Third Street.

GRATIOT AND FARMER STREETS, MAY 29, 1875. Another crowd gathers to witness the laying of another cornerstone, this time for the new Detroit Public Library. The holdings of the library had outgrown the space on the top floor of the Capitol School building and so work began on the new structure.

GRATIOT AND FARMER STREETS, 1877. The new Detroit Public Library building opened for service to the citizens of the city on January 22, 1877. The total cost of the building was $124,000. Over 300 people attended the dedication, presided over by Mayor Lewis. The library was open from seven until ten o'clock that evening.

DETROIT PUBLIC LIBRARY, INTERIOR, 1877. The center of the first floor reading room featured six tables for patrons. Ten large, cast-iron columns rose up from the floor to the roof. The roof was built of iron and stained glass, one-half of an inch thick. Each level of the gallery held 34,000 volumes.

DETROIT PUBLIC LIBRARY, INTERIOR, 1877. The circulation desk of the library featured an electric lamp, while the rest of the library was illuminated by gas jets. There appears to have been magazines or newspapers in the pigeon holes behind the librarian. The marble bust of Lewis Cass at the extreme right can be seen in today's Main Library.

FORT STREET AND SPRINGWELLS, 1870s. Near the city limits on the west side, Harm's Hardware and Tinware shop has a frontier atmosphere and looks as if it belongs in a town in the West rather than a growing city. The business was prospering, as the family was able to add living quarters right next door.

MICHIGAN AVENUE, 1870s. Once known as Michigan Grand Avenue, this thoroughfare was a major access road to points west of the city. Following an old Native American trail, Michigan Avenue was the military road to Chicago. These teamsters appear to be hauling goods for delivery. Note the telegraph poles beginning to sprout up everywhere.

MICHIGAN AVENUE AND TRUMBULL, 1876. This is the hay market, and the wagon loads of hay are parked on the left side of the photo. The DeMan Brothers, Alphonso and Florimand, owned the planing mill and lumber office. This is the northwest corner, which would be turned into a place for baseball in a few short years.

TRUMBULL AND MICHIGAN AVENUES, ON THE NORTH SIDE, 1876. Another scene that looks as if it is out of the Wild West, Trumbull Avenue runs through some as-yet-undeveloped farm lots on the west side of town. Note the handsome buggy in the foreground and the attire of the child on the extreme right.

TROLLEY TRANSPORTATION, 1870S. In 1865, a new company obtained the right to operate through Fort Street from the western limits of the city to Elmwood Avenue. In 1871, the name was changed by a special act of the legislature to the "Fort Wayne and Elmwood Railway Company."

HORSEPOWER DELIVERY, 1870S. The latest in city delivery service, this one-horse model promises express service. The sun roof is optional. There were five major express companies in Detroit, although this one may have been an independent contractor.

ENGINE COMPANY NUMBER THREE, 1871. The latest in fire-fighting equipment—a Phoenix Steam Fire Engine—appears on display at Engine House Number Three on Clifford Street, near Woodward Avenue. Charles McMichael is the foreman and J. Hyland is the engineer. There are three pipe men, one fireman, and a gas company patrolman among this crew.

ENGINE COMPANY NUMBER SIX, 1871. The Detroit Steam Fire Engine Number Six proudly displays what appears to be the same type of fire wagon seen in the previous photo at Russell and High Streets, ready to respond to a call of distress. Peter Ortwine is the foreman, and Peter Smith, the engineer. Warren McCormick is one of the drivers.

SUNDAY MORNING, MAY 18, 1879..   THE DETROIT POST AND TRIBUNE,

CIRCUS.   CIRCUS.   CIRCUS.   CIRCUS.

The Acknowledged Leading Shows of the World.
Gorgeous Cluster of 10 Famous Tented Amusements!
AT DETROIT
For Two Days Only.
WEDNESDAY —AND— THURSDAY, **JUNE 4 & 5**
Location : Corner of Third St. and Grand River Ave.

Also will Exhibit at
Toledo, Saturday, May 31.	Saginaw, Monday, June 9.
Adrian: Monday, June 2.	Flint, Tuesday, June 10.
Jackson, Tuesday, June 3.	Lansing, Wednesday, June 11.
Lapeer, Friday, June 6.	Ionia, Thursday, June 12.
Bay City, Saturday, June 7.	Grand Rapids, Friday, June 13.
	Kalamazoo, Saturday, June 14.

THE ABOVE DATES ARE POSITIVELY CORRECT, AND WILL NOT BE CHANGED.

The World's Famous
Great London Circus & Sangers' English Menagerie
—COMBINED WITH—
The Great International & Australian Allied Shows
COOPER, BAILEY & CO., SOLE OWNERS,
Without any Doubt the Largest and Most Complete Amusement Temple in the World.

DENSE NIGHT
CONVERTED INTO
DAZZLING DAY
By the Brush
DYNAMO ELECTRIC-LIGHT !
18 ELECTRIC
Light CHANDELIERS
Equal to 35,000 Gas Jets.

—REQUIRING—
40-Horse Power Boiler,
30-Horse-Power Engine,
900 Revolutions a Minute,
28,000 Yards
INSULATED CABLE
WIRE.

Burning Brilliantly under Water.   In Operation Night and Day.
Glowing with a Phosphorescent Effulgence.   Equal to the Rays of Four Dazzling Suns.
Illuminating a Radius of Two Miles.   A Steel File Melted in an Instant, yet No Heat.

Worth Traveling 500 Miles to See the Wondrous Light in Operation.
10   OUR HERD OF ELEPHANTS.   10

DETROIT POST AND TRIBUNE, MAY 18, 1879. The circus is coming to town! To this day a major attraction in any city, the traveling circus began its heyday during the 1870s. This one comes from London, England. The interesting attraction is the new electric light display which will "convert dense night into dazzling day."

HERE COME THE ELEPHANTS! The Great London Circus and Sangers English Menagerie makes its way down to the grounds at Third Street and Grand River Avenue for its two-day Detroit engagement. The circus will travel to ten Michigan cities by the end of June and has just arrived from Jackson.

Three

The 1880s

MARVIN H. CHAMBERLAIN—MAYOR OF DETROIT, 1885–1886. Born in Woodstock Township, Lenawee County, in 1842, Chamberlain graduated from Adrian College in 1864. In 1865 he entered the wholesale liquor business, and his firm became one of the largest in Michigan. In 1874 he helped organize the Michigan Commercial Travelers Association and was its first president. Chamberlain was one of the first 12 councilmen elected when that board was created in 1881 and was elected its president in 1885. In 1883 he was defeated in his bid for mayor as a Democratic candidate, before winning the job in 1885. Chamberlain built one of the first plants for the reduction of garbage collected in Detroit and built similar plants in other cities under patents he controlled. He governed a city of 116,340 souls.

A VIEW OF DETROIT FROM WINDSOR, CANADA, 1880. This rare photograph shows Detroit in the distance across the river. The tremendous growth of the city in the past decade is evident from the emerging skyline. In the middle, in the distance, is pictured one of the excursion steamers that plied the river from Detroit to Belle Isle. In the foreground is a Canadian boat at the Windsor dock.

RIVERFRONT BETWEEN GRISWOLD AND SHELBY STREETS, 1880. Just west of Woodward Avenue, this section of riverfront shows two travel steamers belonging to Stephen B. Grummond, who also owned tugboats. These vessels ran from Detroit to Port Huron. On the extreme left is a commercial sail vessel used for moving goods around the Great Lakes.

WOODWARD AND JEFFERSON AVENUES, 1881. Soper's Cigar Store, owned and operated by Horace U. Soper, occupied the northeast corner of the intersection. F.S. Stenton's hat shop stood at 177 Jefferson Avenue, and the central office for the Association of Charities was around the corner heading up Woodward.

CAMPUS MARTIUS, 1881. The new Detroit Opera House opened in 1876. On the ground floor Joseph L. Hudson opened his own clothing store after working for the C.R. Mabley men's clothing store for five years. The jewelry store on the left would become the Wright, Kay & Company, while the Hull Brothers grocers would be destroyed in a fire in 1893, with the Opera House burning as well.

WOODWARD AND GRAND RIVER AVENUES, 1881. The 100 block of Woodward near Grand River had George M. Travers's dry goods store at 111 and 113 Woodward, right next to Abraham Heller clothing at 125. C.R. Mabley's furniture show room is visible at 127 and 129—his clothing store was across the street. Walter Buhl, who sells hats, caps, and furs, was related to former mayor Christian Buhl.

CONGRESS AND GRISWOLD STREETS, 1881. The northeast corner of the intersection had a couple of bookstores, one new and one used. Sandwiched in between was the Charles E. Letts Coal Office and the Eclectic Life Insurance Company of New York. The Federal Post Office is on the extreme right.

WOODWARD AVENUE BETWEEN THE DOCKS AND ATWATER STREET, 1880s. What better place for a saloon, restaurant, and dining room owned by a well-known name than just down the street from where you got off the boat? The Western Union establishment was run by Michael Dowd at 10 Woodward. Alongside is the inevitable hat factory.

THE CENTRAL MARKET, 1885. This is a view of the market at Cadillac Square, but this time with the addition of that two-spired building in the middle, seen in the distance. Built in 1881, this structure had market stalls on the ground floor, while on the upper floor were some city departments.

WOODWARD AVENUE NEAR GRAND RIVER, 1885. The west side of the Avenue at 122 to 134 is the big C.R. Mabley clothing and shoe store. Across the street was his furniture store. Here are two elegant buggies parked outside which may reflect on the clientele inside. It would appear that James Scott actually owned or erected the building itself.

WOODWARD AVENUE BETWEEN STATE AND MICHIGAN, 1887. J.L. Hudson opened up his second store in 1887 in this location just around the corner from Campus Martius. This entire building was devoted to his store, the first of many expansions. Soon he would move from this spot to another way up town at Gratiot and Farmer Streets.

WOODWARD AND GRATIOT AVENUES, 1887. Frederick Rolshoven's jewelry store anchors this corner at 70 Woodward. Mouat & Sheley sold gas fixtures and, as the city basically ran on natural gas, did quite well in business. The First Presbyterian Church was built in 1854, and at the extreme right is the Finney Hotel.

CAMPUS MARTIUS, 1888. A beautiful, panoramic view of the heart of downtown Detroit, this shot, from in front of the new Central Market building, shows the city gearing up for the start of some event as a crowd gathers. The new city hall dominates the photo on the left, while advertising for Hudson's dominates the right.

WOODWARD AND MICHIGAN AVENUES, 1880s. Hott's *A Texas Steer* was playing at the Detroit Opera House when Fred Sanders opened his ice cream parlor. With its distinguishing, onion-shaped dome, it would be a cool spot for Detroiters to relax for years to come.

MICHIGAN AVENUE, 1880s. A one-horsepower streetcar makes its way into town from the west side. Just above it is August Elkey's beer hall, at 536 Michigan. There are just a few gas lights along this stretch of Michigan, but more telegraph/telephone poles. Note the attire of the woman and boy on the extreme right.

WOODWARD AVENUE AND ADAMS STREET, 1881. William H. Dewey's Ice Cream and Oyster House (some combination) occupied the corner here. The store is evidently doing well enough to employ a horse and delivery wagon to add catering to its business. This north Woodward area in Grand Circus Park was still partly residential, but would not remain so for long.

LAFAYETTE BOULEVARD, 1880S. Patrick Blake stands proudly but solemnly in front of his establishment at 25 and 27 Lafayette. Detroiters were taken on their last trip in this elegant hearse. Blake and his family lived on the premises. There were at least 14 undertakers in the city and none were more strategically placed than this one next to Drake's Homeopathic Pharmacy.

THIRD AND WOODBRIDGE STREETS, 1880S. The Michigan Central Railroad shared this depot with the Grand Trunk. Looking north along Third Street is Thomas Quinn's saloon, at the intersection of Congress is Thomas McGregor's Boiler Works, and all the way up to Fort Street is the Fort Street Presbyterian Church.

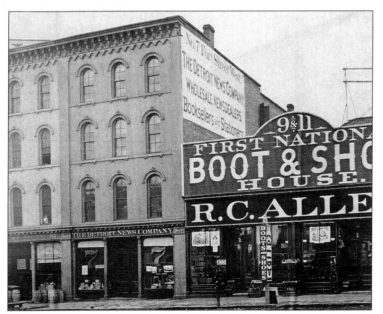

FORT STREET, JUST WEST OF WOODWARD, 1880S. The Detroit News Company at 7 West Fort Street were wholesale news dealers, booksellers, and stationers, managed by Joseph A. Marsh, who was also the treasurer. They would start issuing their own newspaper, the *Evening News*, in 1873. The inevitable shoe store is owned by Rollin C. Allen.

THE MICHIGAN STOVE COMPANY, 1889. One of Detroit's leading manufacturing organizations was the Michigan Stove Company. They manufactured a number of products, such as this Garland Stove. Among others was the Art Stove and the Jewel Range. They later merged with the Detroit Stove Works and became the Michigan Stove Works.

THE "HOME-GARLAND," 1889.

THE WORLD'S BEST.

The Standard Wood Cooking Stove of the World.

Leads all Others in Sales and Popularity.

MAY BE HAD WITHOUT ORNAMENTAL LEG BASE IF DESIRED.

"Aluminum" is mixed with the iron from which all "Garland" Stoves and Ranges are made.

THE MICHIGAN STOVE COMPANY,

THE MICHIGAN STOVE COMPANY, 1880s. Proudly posing in front of their building at 1024 Jefferson Avenue, corner of Adair, the entire working force showed off some of their products. Mr. Francis Palms was the president of the company. The success of the industry was evident in the fact that "stove money" founded several Detroit banks.

GRISWOLD AVENUE, 1880S. The staff of the Detroit Stained Glass Works posed in front of their building at 109 Griswold. Charles Fredericks and Peter Staffin were the proprietors. These glass stainers made their products for church dwellings, steamboats, and railroad cars. They would send samples for churches free of charge. The man standing third from the right was a French artist named Ignatuis Schott.

WOODWARD AVENUE, 1880S. This gigantic pipe was produced by the Russell Wheel and Foundry Company, located on the river at the foot of Walker Street, on the east side. George H. and Walter S. Russell were the proprietors. This pipe was destined to become part of the sewer system.

ELIJAH McCOY, 1880s. Born in Colchester, Canada, in 1844, Elijah McCoy was sent to Scotland in 1859 to study engineering at the University of Edinburgh. In 1865 he decided to seek his fortune with the Michigan Central Railroad in Ypsilanti. Forced to take a job as a fireman, he never lost his inquisitiveness and always tinkered with the machinery around him.

OIL LUBRICATION DEVICE. One of at least 50 patents in his name, this device was one of the first. This invention would automatically lubricate an engine, in this case a railroad engine. The device was patented in 1872 and installed on all of the Michigan Central Railroad engines. Elijah McCoy moved to Detroit in 1882.

GRATIOT AVENUE, 1882. The Lion Brewery Company at 331 Gratiot was run by the Stroh family—Bernard (junior and senior), Emil, Fred, and Julius. They would soon put their family name on their product. On the far right is the Trinity (German) Lutheran Church, a new building erected in 1867, in the German-dominated east side.

GRAND RIVER AND CHERRY STREET, 1880S. There were over 30 brewers in the city of Detroit during the 1880s. Edward W. Voight was the proprietor of this one in the 200 block of Grand River Avenue, producing Rhinegold Beer. Note the several different types of delivery vehicles employed at that time.

MICHIGAN AVENUE, 1881. The ice cream wagon fleet belongs to Joseph M. Flinn and Alanson Durfee. The firm of Flinn & Durfee also made and wholesaled butter and cheese, and dealt in milk, canned fruit, and oysters. That is the Waterloo Yeast Company on the far left, with Thomas W. Filer as manager.

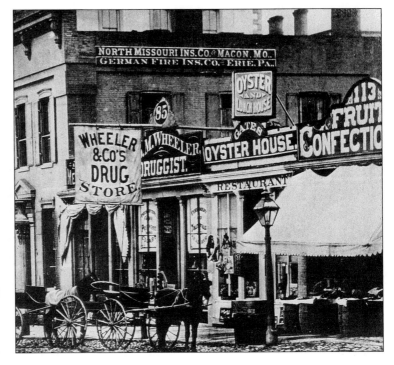

GRISWOLD, NORTH OF CONGRESS STREET, 1885. The diversity of the city businesses is plain to see in this photograph of Griswold—John Hanrahan's fruit and confectionery store, next to Gates's oyster house, next to Wheeler's drugstore, followed by two insurance companies.

WOODWARD AVENUE, 1880s. An interesting diversion for Detroiters was the opportunity to look at sunspots through this man's telescope—despite the risk of damage to the eyes which could be caused by such an act. Note the unique traveling cart for his equipment. It would be interesting to know how much he charged for this diversion.

DETROIT FIRE DEPARTMENT, 1884. This latest in steam-powered, fire-fighting equipment is the one and only, self-propelled, steam fire engine in the department. This machine is an Amoskeag, built in New Hampshire. It weighed 5 tons, had a top speed of 15 miles per hour, and cost $5,000. It was called "Hercules."

EAST FOREST AVENUE, 1880s. Certified milk, with the quality service from the Belle Isle Creamery Company, was brought to your door each morning. Belle Isle milk was "the First Food of Life" and "the Most Economical." Quite a few businesses took this name from the island—there was never actually a creamery or dairy on it.

SEVENTEENTH STREET NEAR HOWARD, 1881. Named after an old, prominent Detroit family, the Trowbridge School offered more than one classroom, having added a second floor. There were three teachers employed there: Miss Harriet C. Park (principal), Miss Emma J. Harrington, and Miss Anna C. Trakey. Mr. Henry M. Utley was acting president and secretary of the board of education.

FORT STREET, CORNER OF FIFTH, 1881. At 264 Fort Street stood the home of Alexander Delano, who was the treasurer and manager of the Detroit Car Spring Company, a company that manufactured steel railway car springs. His office was in the Moffat Building and the works were located at Michigan Avenue and Bay City Crossing.

WOODWARD AVENUE AND HANCOCK, 1881. On the southeast corner stood the residence of Richard H. Fyfe, who was the president of Fyfe Boots and Shoes. Born in New York and raised in Hillsdale County, he came to Detroit in 1857 and began working in the retail shoe business. In 1865, he started a shoe business of his own, which grew to be one of the largest in the country.

THE "BILL" AT WHITNEY'S, FEBRUARY 12, 1885. These two humorists took turns introducing each other and gave renditions of their works—not just readings of their published pieces, but renditions, with the novelists often acting out each part in the particular piece. Note the nautical play on "Mark Twain Cable" Readings.

WHITNEY'S OPERA HOUSE.

Thursday Evening, Feb. 12th, 1885.

THE

"Mark Twain" Cable Readings.

PROGRAMME.

1. RAOUL INNERARITY EXHIBITS HIS PAINTING.
   GEO. W. CABLE.
2. DESPERATE ENCOUNTER WITH AN INTERVIEWER.
   MARK TWAIN.
3. RAOUL INNERARITY ANNOUNCES HIS MARRIAGE.
   GEO. W. CABLE.
4. TOM SAWYER AND HUCK FINN'S BRILLIANT ACHIEVEMENTS.
   MARK TWAIN.
5. AMORE AND HONORE—COURTSHIP SCENE.
   GEO. W. CABLE.
6. THE BLUE JAY'S MISTAKE.
   MARK TWAIN.
7. MARY'S NIGHT RIDE.
   GEO. W. CABLE.
8. THE JUMPING FROG.
   MARK TWAIN.

FORT STREET AND SHELBY, 1885. On the northwest corner stood Clark J. Whitney's Grand Opera House. The location was one block from Griswold Street and city hall and had a frontage of 96 feet on Fort Street and 136 feet on Shelby. It had steam heat and elevators to every floor.

RIVER SCENE, 1880s. A Sunday excursion for some Detroiters was to the riverfront, where a family could picnic and watch the traffic on the river. This family was able to see an 1880s version of the "tall ships" sailing gracefully down river. This may be a scene from Belle Isle.

ANOTHER RIVER SCENE, 1880s. If watching was not your style, you could always be on the river yourself, as these rowing crews were preparing to do. These young ladies, who appear to be wearing the same type of clothing, are ready for a brisk session. The gentleman in front will keep the rowers in unison by calling out the stroke.

BRADY STREET, BETWEEN JOHN R. AND BRUSH, 1880. This is a photograph of Detroit's premiere sporting park looking toward the baseball field from the half-mile point of the racetrack for horses; an amateur game or practice is in progress. In the middle, in the distance, is the grandstand, and on the left is the back of the front gate.

AMATEUR BASEBALL, 1889. One of the many amateur teams was this solemn-looking group of players made up of Detroit's finest. One of the requirements may have been a good-sized handlebar moustache. Note the early equipment—bats and catchers mask. The manager is in the middle, dressed in his uniform—a proper suit.

BRADY STREET, 1880s. Here is the front gate of what was known as Recreation Park. Large enough to hold two Tiger Stadiums, baseball admission was 50¢, reserved seats 75¢, and season tickets were $25 for 63 home dates in 1887. Frederick Stearns owned the team.

RECREATION PARK, 1880s. This is the back side of the front gate at the horse racing track. There is a mixed crowd of ladies and sporting gentlemen and some children waiting for the event to begin. Note the observation platform that extends out from the second floor to enable spectators and race officials to observe the entire race.

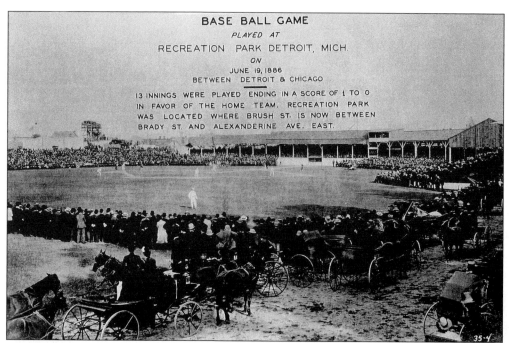

BASE BALL GAME
PLAYED AT
RECREATION PARK DETROIT, MICH.
ON
JUNE 19, 1886
BETWEEN DETROIT & CHICAGO

13 INNINGS WERE PLAYED ENDING IN A SCORE OF 1 TO 0
IN FAVOR OF THE HOME TEAM. RECREATION PARK
WAS LOCATED WHERE BRUSH ST. IS NOW BETWEEN
BRADY ST. AND ALEXANDERINE AVE. EAST.

35-4

RECREATION PARK, 1886. The Detroit Baseball Club joined the National League in 1886 and played their home games here. This is a rare photograph of a game in progress on June 19, 1886, versus Chicago. The game ended after 13 innings in a one to nothing shutout victory for the Detroits. Note the new grandstand and the absence of a racetrack.

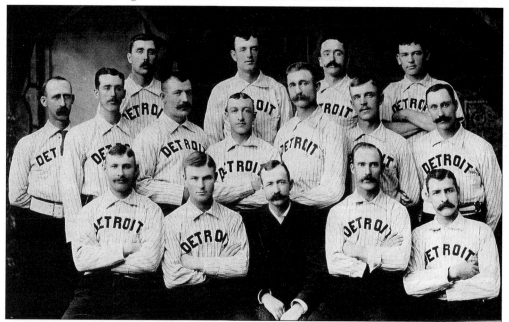

WORLD CHAMPIONS, 1887. This formal portrait of the champions shows off their uniforms, which were patterned after the uniforms of volunteer firemen. The team finished with a record of 79 wins and 45 losses. First baseman Dan Brouthers and right fielder Sam Thompson both hit over .400 that year and would end up in the Hall of Fame.

DETROIT RIVER DOCKS, 1889. This Detroit couple is waiting for the boat to take them down river to the Detroit International Fair and Exposition, which was held from September 17 to September 27, 1889. Queen Anne Soap was a popular product made locally by the Detroit Soap Company.

DETROIT RIVER AT THE ROUGE RIVER, 1889. This was the main boat landing at the river entrance to the International Fair and Exposition. Ferryboats ran daily from Port Huron, Detroit, and Canada, carrying passengers to and from the fair. These folks are waiting for transportation, while two water wagons manage to keep the dust down by lightly spraying the roads.

DETROIT RIVER, JUST SOUTH OF FORT WAYNE, 1889. This photograph depicts the other boat landing that was directly on the Detroit River. These people had a three- or four-block riverfront stroll to the main entrance. There were streetcar, electric railway, and railroad lines set up from the city to the fair, which was located not one thousand yards from the city limit.

INTERNATIONAL EXPOSITION, 1889. The main exhibit building on the fairgrounds looked like a European fortress or palace. It had a frontage of 500 feet and an exhibit area of 200,000 square feet. The central tower rose to 200 feet and there were 4.5 acres of glass in its walls. It was the largest exhibit building in the world.

THE INTERNATIONAL FAIR, 1889. There were many attractions available on the grounds outside of the main pavilion. One of these was of the Wild West variety, as this cowboy marksman takes aim at a stationary target. The fair was a combination agricultural and industrial event, as well as an exposition.

THE INTERNATIONAL EXPOSITION, 1889. It looks as though this hot-air balloon is not going to clear one of the main building towers, although that may have been the plan—to see how close one could get. Events such as these lent a carnival atmosphere to the exposition.

THE INTERNATIONAL FAIR, 1889. Special train and streetcar lines and steamship lines were all set up to see to the needs of the visitors to the fair. Their medical needs were seen to as well, as this temporary first-aid station suggests. It was set up and staffed by Harper Hospital personnel. The fair was so large that it probably deserved a two- or three-day visit.

THE DETROIT INTERNATIONAL EXPOSITION, 1889. A give-away map of the fairgrounds shows its location just south of Fort Wayne and the extent of its size—14 acres in area. The oval track and water basins on the right were used for harness racing and sailing races. Baseball and lacrosse contests were also staged here. The site was used for expositions through 1892.

FORT AND GRISWOLD STREETS, 1889. A beautiful view looking west down Fort Street shows the wide, clean streets and different styles and sizes of buildings. The tall structure on the extreme left is the Hammond Building, and on the right is the Moffat Building. Both buildings contained a number of offices for lawyers, real estate agents, small businesses, and insurance companies. Nearly all of the office space was always leased. Farther down on the left is the Detroit Club and the Grace Episcopal Church, while on the right is the Fort Street Presbyterian Church, the Union Depot grounds, and the home of Russell Alger. Note the various forms of transportation: foot, wagon, and electric railway. Each building also had its own lightning rod.

Four

The 1890s

HAZEN S. PINGREE—MAYOR OF DETROIT, 1889–1895. Born in Maine, Pingree was convinced to come to Detroit while a guest of the Confederate government at Andersonville Prison. The son of a shoemaker, he went into that business in 1866 and later formed a partnership with Charles H. Smith. By 1889, they had annual sales of $1 million, and Pingree grudgingly accepted the Republican nomination for mayor. Hazen Pingree was a reform mayor well before muckraking began and was always a champion of the common man. He first offered reform in public utilities and transportation as well as repaving the city's streets with stone or asphalt on a permanent base. He lowered the streetcar fare from 5¢ to 3¢ and carried on the fight for reform for the next seven years.

THE FOOT OF WOODWARD AT THE RIVER, 1890. This is a scene from mid-river, looking straight up Woodward Avenue. To the right are some small boats at the dock, while to the left is one of the pleasure steamers that plied the river from Wyandotte to Port Huron. Some horse trolleys are lined up at the dock ready for their return ride north. Note the tall light towers used for illumination at night.

WOODWARD AND JEFFERSON AVENUES, 1890. A close-up of this busy intersection shows the telegraph and electric wires starting to bloom in the city. On the extreme right is one of the last horse-drawn trolleys, while on the left is a waiting line of hansoms and taxis.

WOODWARD AVENUE AND CONGRESS, 1890. Moving farther north up Woodward, there are many more wires; bigger, more permanent-looking buildings; and the same types of transportation. In the middle foreground is a person on a bicycle, a conveyance gaining rapidly in popularity. The Mabley & Company building and the Russell House are on the east side of the street.

WOODWARD AVENUE, NEAR CAMPUS MARTIUS, 1890s. A closer view of the area in the previous photograph shows some of the very first electric streetcars on the Woodward line. It now became a little more hazardous to cross the street. A better view is had of the light tower on the extreme right, which cast a faint light on the street below.

MICHIGAN AND WOODWARD AVENUES, 1890S. The northwest corner of these two busy streets shows some of the latest fashions that both men and women wore during the "Gay '90s." The man in the left-center of the picture looks a little cross, while behind him there is quite a crowd in front of Sanders.

ON THE AVENUE, 1890S. Woodward Avenue was the street to show off the finest women's fashions. An excellent illustration of women's and girls' clothing, these Detroiters stroll in front of Rolshoven's Jewelers, which appears to have had a large clock at the corner of its entrance. Next door is an outlet selling Garland and Jewel stoves.

WOODWARD AVENUE, 1890S. A new building erected on Woodward just north of Michigan was the Home Savings Bank. Various delivery wagons were transporting goods to and from businesses daily. One can see the trolley tracks laid down the middle of the street.

STATE STREET AND WOODWARD AVENUE, 1890S. This magnificent, white horse seems to know his picture is being taken as he holds his head up proudly. More fashions are seen here, and a baby carriage is just visible between the ladies. The drugstore is selling mineral water and ginger ale and is also festooned with bunting in honor of some event.

CAMPUS MARTIUS, 1890s.
This elegantly dressed
gentleman makes his way across
Campus Martius, possibly
heading toward his lodgings in
the Russell House. The
Michigan Phonograph
Company now shared space on
the ground floor of the Opera
House with a bank, and the
Hudson store had its own
building. The Wright,
Kay & Company jewelers was
next door.

WOODWARD AVENUE, 1890s.
Another example of men's
fashions is apparent in this
photograph. This gentleman has
his bowler and walking stick and
appears confident that he will
retain his headgear on this
windy day. The Sanders ice
cream store is barely visible on
the far right.

CADILLAC SQUARE, 1890S. This man pauses from his labor to pose for this picture. A hay wagon makes its way to the central market, just visible on the far left. The building with all of the awnings is the Russell House. There appears to be some street construction going on here.

CADILLAC SQUARE, 1890S. This is a busy street scene as these Detroiters shop along Cadillac Square. One can almost smell the aromas from the open-air markets, especially Ward and Wingert's fish, oyster, and game market. The Marx Brothers, Adolph and Benjamin, ran the butcher shop. The Salvation Army Headquarters was at 21 New Central Market.

CADILLAC SQUARE, 1894. The heart of the market district in the north central part of the city had a variety of different markets and amusements. Right above the central meat market was Sweeney's billiard room. It seems that every town had a Sweeney's. Both business and the latest in gossip were discussed in the middle of the street.

GRISWOLD AND MICHIGAN AVENUE, 1892. This photograph was taken in August and shows another busy day in the expanding business district. *Kentucky Girl* was playing at Whitney's Grand Opera House, ladies' watches were an expensive $17.50 at Van Baalen's pawnbrokers, and the Martin Brothers were in business selling banners, signs, and portraits.

WOODWARD AVENUE, SOUTH FROM GRATIOT, 1890s. The west side of Woodward heading south toward the river now had a number of new businesses. Hugo Hill owned a large millinery, and Weber furniture was in stiff competition with Mabley's. The growth of the city is evident by the sign for the British and American Employment Office. The dentist next door offered vitalized air teeth.

WOODWARD AVENUE BETWEEN MICHIGAN AVENUE AND STATE STREET, 1890s. This photo is a good shot taken across the square, toward C.J. Whitney's music store, a longtime Detroit landmark. William H. Elliott's Dry Goods House is to the left. Heyn's Bazaar, owned by Emil Heyn, Henry Binswanger, and John G. Meyer, is to the right.

WOODWARD AVENUE, 1890s. A rush for the trolley captures these citizens in the course of their daily business. The two ladies in the foreground wear the latest in '90s fashions. The lady just above them wears a more sedate apparel. The men seem to be dressed alike, with straw boaters—the latest in headgear.

WOODWARD AVENUE, LOOKING SOUTH FROM JEFFERSON, 1895. Down the center of the street ran one of the first electric trolley cars to operate in the city. It would share track space with the horse-drawn variety until after the turn of the century. Detroit streets were beginning to become crowded.

WOODWARD AVENUE AT CAMPUS MARTIUS, 1895. At what might be called the heart of town was the hustle and bustle of a city on the move. In the right foreground is the lawn in front of city hall. A line of coaches is waiting to pick up their passengers. Across the street is the Central Market building, which had some city offices on the upper floors.

WOODWARD AVENUE, NORTH OF CAMPUS MARTIUS, 1890s. The expansion of the city northward can be seen in this photograph as businesses extend farther and farther up the avenue, pushing residential areas ahead of them. A policeman leans against the telephone pole to the left, and the large pair of eyeglasses on the right indicates an optician's office.

CAMPUS MARTIUS, 1890S. A close view of the Soldiers and Sailors Monument shows that the second set of statues has yet to be added. Another new clothing store, the Star, occupies ground floor space on the Woodward corner. The fountain on the west side of the street sat in front of city hall.

CAMPUS MARTIUS, 1895. The Soldiers and Sailors Monument is now complete with statuary on every tier. The overhead electrical wires are in place for the streetcars. *Rob Roy* is playing at the Opera House, which has a new occupant, the National Loan Investment Company. The streets are paved with brick.

JEFFERSON AVENUE AT ATWATER STREET, 1890S. This barefoot young man treads lightly over brick pavers as he crosses Jefferson Avenue close to the river. The electrical wires are up for the street railway, and one can see the variety of businesses down near the dock area.

HOWARD STREET, 1895. The combination of old residences and businesses is shown in this photograph of a near west side street. Some of the old homes are starting to show their age and would soon be replaced by new buildings. These homes seem to have been used to hang advertising posters.

MICHIGAN AND WOODWARD AVENUES, 1895. This was the site of Fred Sanders's first ice cream parlor and was razed to make way for the new Mabley and Company building, which would be 14 stories high. As the sign claims, it was to be the highest commercial building and department store in Michigan.

WOODWARD AVENUE, JUST SOUTH OF CAMPUS MARTIUS, 1890S. A growing and prosperous city needs to have better-paved and wider streets. This is the scene on Woodward Avenue in the mid-1890s. These teamsters may have been hauling paving materials while citizens looked on and tried to stay out of the mud.

THE FORT WAYNE TROLLEY LINE, 1890S. This homemade apparatus is being used to install the electrical lines for the Fort Wayne streetcar line as the city becomes more and more electrified. In this scene, on a street just west of Woodward, are some of the early electric poles.

GRISWOLD STREET, LOOKING NORTH, 1897. The downtown area of the city has taken a more recognizable shape by the end of the decade. It is completely business oriented, with the residential areas located more toward the city limits. The Buhl Block is on the left and the Telegraph Block is on the right of the photograph.

WOODWARD AVENUE, 1890S. The J. Black Carpet Company can be seen in the middle of the photo, in the distance, to the left of Wright, Kay & Company. This line of taxis is probably parked in front of city hall. This photograph provides another good look at the fashions of the day and the light towers which rose to over 100 feet above the streets.

WOODWARD AND MICHIGAN AVENUES, 1890S. This serenely dressed matron makes her way across the street in front of the Farnsworth shoe store. This side of the intersection was anchored by the two photograph galleries for many years. Farnsworth would soon move to larger quarters, having been in this location since 1881.

WOODWARD AND WITHERELL, 1895. This view looking south along Woodward Avenue shows the Smith, Sturgeon & Company jewelers, which shared building space with Annis Furs. The three-story, light-colored building between Smith's and Goldberg's Dry Goods houses James Vernor's drugstore. Note the fashionably dressed lady and the natural gas light post, both with protective covering.

JEFFERSON AVENUE EAST, 1890s. The Allen Brothers, William and Orville, opened a new store at 247 East Jefferson that included a new product called Kodak. Fred Bamford and Company offered interior decorating supplies, including some locally produced stained glass. It looks as though Jefferson Avenue was in need of some repaving.

BETHUNE AVENUE, 1898. Some of Detroit's finest proudly pose in front of their new station on Bethune in the late 1890s. Members of the newly formed, mounted section are also here. The stables are to the right of the photograph. The men are wearing a "Keystones Kops"-type of helmet, then in use.

THE BLACK MARIA, 1890s. One of Detroit's famous paddy wagons, called the "Black Maria," is pictured here. Detroit was the second city to use a vehicle to transport its officers to their beats and prisoners to the station houses. The wagons were located at just a few of the stations, including headquarters.

WOODWARD AVENUE, 1892. A welcoming arch stretches across Woodward in anticipation of the arrival of the Grand Army of the Republic (GAR), for their annual encampment. The GAR was the first veterans organization made up of the Union veterans of the Civil War. The Mabley Bazaar is on the left and the second J.L. Hudson store is in the middle in the distance.

WOODWARD AVENUE, 1892. This is a view looking north along the street at the same arch but from the other side. The nine symbols hanging from the arch represent nine Union Army Corps badges, to one of which every GAR member belonged while on active service. The three portraits represent Union generals. The city is festooned with red, white, and blue.

CITY HALL, 1892. All of the surviving participants of the Civil War were invited to Detroit during the summer of 1892. The city hall was one place for registration of veterans. States represented by the vets included Illinois, Michigan, and Wisconsin. The view is looking to the northwest with Fort Street in the foreground.

GAR REUNION, 1892. This is a more traditional triumphal arch, unfortunately on an unidentifiable street. Two Union eagles flank a portrait of a Civil War battle scene. This monument was undoubtedly taller. Some of the veterans can be seen in the shot, their dress and mannerisms a give-away. Note the man holding his umbrella like a musket.

GAR REUNION, 1892. Nearly every regiment in the Civil War army had its own band. Here one group of veteran musicians gives an impromptu concert in front of one of the city's residences. Civil War music was certainly played, but some bands could be coaxed into playing the more modern tunes.

GAR REUNION, 1892. Yet another type of triumphal arch somewhere along Woodward or Jefferson Avenues, this one was roped by garland and topped by live plants. It is rather ornate, with its columns and railings for a temporary memorial. All of these decorations were in place prior to the grand parade.

WOODWARD AVENUE, SUMMER, 1892. The final parade of the Grand Army of the Republic is seen here as it passes in review down Woodward. The men are in uniform, some even wearing their knapsacks as they march by regiment. Some officers are on horseback and the surviving regimental colors are proudly carried by color bearers.

GAR REUNION, 1892. One final look at a fourth example of an arch, this one was flanked by cannon and bedecked by the national flag. The symbols on the arch represent every corps in the Union Army. This photograph shows a nice example of a fruit vendor's wagon and three of those newfangled bicycles. A group of veterans appear to be waiting for a start under the arch to the left.

MAYOR'S OFFICE, 1892. This is a rare photograph of city officials inside the mayor's office at city hall. The mayor, Hazen Pingree, is leaning against the chair conversing to two others, probably about cleaning up after the reunion. The fourth man, to the right, appears as a ghostly image beneath the portrait of Governor Stevens T. Mason.

BOARD OF PUBLIC WORKS, 1890s. The fleet of horse-drawn Board of Public Works (BPW) street cleaners lines up for review before heading out to "clean up" the city. As is evident from these photographs, they did a fairly good job.

FOOT OF WOODWARD, RIVER DOCKS, 1890S. An inexpensive form of recreation for Detroiters was an excursion on the river, even if it was just a short boat ride to Belle Isle Park. Families could enjoy a picnic lunch and watch river traffic from the island. This ticket office at the foot of Woodward maintained a steady business.

ALL ABOARD FOR THE ISLAND, 1890S. Here is a group of Detroiters waiting to board one of the excursion steamers and sail to Belle Isle. This particular boat should look familiar to all Detroiters, as it resembles the type of vessel that will run up and down the river to Bob-Lo. Note the latest fashions of the time.

BELLE ISLE, 1890S. These young ladies could be on a trip from school, as they seem to be in a segregated and chaperoned group. The older girl standing next to the adult appears reluctant to bare her ankles and wade in.

BELLE ISLE, 1890S. More fun is had on the beach on the island. Either it is not quite warm enough to swim, or no one thought to bring a suit. It won't be too long before this young man is in long pants. That is the Detroit Boat Club on the extreme right.

DETROIT RIVER DOCKS, 1890S. The White Star Line Wharf along the riverfront was always one of the city's busiest, with passenger arrivals and departures during most of the sailing season. They not only did a good business, but provided non-passengers with an event to witness. These boats sailed along all the Great Lakes.

THE RIVERFRONT, 1890S. For the more adventurous sailor, the river provided an excellent means to practice navigation and improve strength and stamina through rowing. These family groups seem to be docking after a full day's pleasure. This scene appears to be taking place a little farther down river.

WOODWARD AVENUE AND JOHN R. STREET, 1890S. The east side of the street between Gratiot and Grand Circus Park offered a variety of goods and services, including a new music store—Grinnell Brothers. There are a lot of photographers' studios, including Tomlinson's—the photographer of the Detroit Wolverines Baseball Club.

WOODWARD AVENUE BETWEEN STATE AND GRAND RIVER, 1890S. Detroit seemed to be full of dry goods merchants and milliners. Here is the Charles F. Pennewell & Company, which also sold draperies. The Zickel Brothers, Harry H. and Edward, sold and published music as well as instruments.

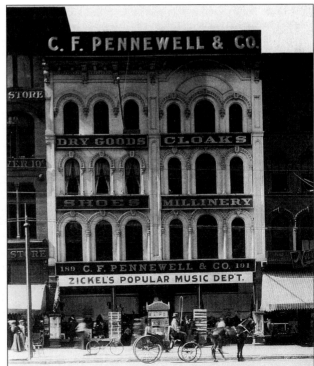

113

LAFAYETTE BOULEVARD AND SHELBY STREET, 1895. On the northwest corner of the intersection stood Philharmonic Hall, one of several concert halls in a music-loving city. This particular building was done in the Greek style and was known for its excellent acoustics.

DETROIT NEWSBOY BAND, 1890S. Detroit has always had more than its share of bands, but they were never more popular than during the 1890s. Practically every organization had a band—the fire and police departments, the local militia, the 4th United States Infantry, and the Detroit Newsboys, to name a few. They played concerts and attended band competitions.

WOODWARD AVENUE AND LARNED STREET, 1890S. One of the most popular city attractions was the Wonderland Musee and Theater, located at 80 Woodward, on the southeast corner at Larned. James H. Moore and Enoch W. Wiggins, proprietor and manager, would hold just about any kind of entertainment here, from concerts to zoo exhibits.

EAST JEFFERSON AVENUE AND PENNSYLVANIA STREET, 1890S. The entrance to Waterworks Park is dominated by the Hurlbut Memorial Gate. Mr. Chauncey Hurlbut made a fortune in the grocery trade and later worked to improve the water system in the city. He was appointed city water commissioner in 1861, and on his death in 1885 bequeathed his estate to the water commission for a library and grounds improvement.

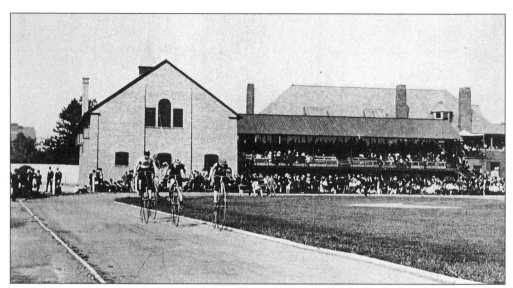

WOODWARD AVENUE BETWEEN CANFIELD AND FOREST, 1890S. Bicycle races, among other things, were held on the grounds of the Detroit Athletic Club. This was a major sport during the decade, as can be seen from the crowd. Some popular racers were Major Taylor, Eddie "Cannonball" Bald, and Detroit's own, Tom Cooper.

WASHINGTON AVENUE, NORTH OF GRAND RIVER, 1890S. Perhaps the epitome of the bicycle craze is this monster, the "Oriten," made in Waltham, Massachusetts. The only bicycle in the world that was built for ten riders, it weighed 305 pounds and had a carrying capacity of 2,500 pounds. Its top speed was 1 mile in 1 minute and 20 seconds.

HERE THEY COME! Detroiters line the streets to see another circus parade. Watched over by one of the city's finest, the traveling circus was one of the summer's more popular events. Photos like these offer an excellent opportunity to see the people and fashions of the day.

WASHINGTON BOULEVARD, 1890s. Always the stars of the show are the elephants, as the circus moves from the train station to the waiting circus grounds. Most of the people pictured here are children, as it should be, and a group of boys are following immediately after the elephant. One can almost feel the excitement.

WOODWARD AVENUE AT CAMPUS MARTIUS, 1895. A grand parade proceeds right down through the heart of the city in dedication of the new Masonic Temple, located at the southeast corner of First Street and Lafayette Boulevard. One can see the Masonic band and a contingent of the Knights Templar in their distinctive uniforms.

WOODWARD AVENUE AT FORT STREET, 1896. It seems as though the city used any excuse to have a celebration and parade. This "float" represents the ship *Result* and was part of the Evacuation Day festivities. July 11th was the date of the arrival in Detroit of United States troops under General Anthony Wayne and the withdrawal of the British garrison in 1796.

EVACUATION DAY, JULY 11, 1896. What parade of homemade floats would be complete without the participation of the children. These two darlings have their own wagon, complete with flag and advertising, drawn by a perfectly matched set of goats. Note the other type of cobblestone street.

WOODWARD AVENUE, 1890S. Detroiters could pride themselves on their clean city streets. These workers from the Board of Public Works look like they are in parade formation. The president of the board was Dewey Moreland, and these men were known as his "white wings" because of their spotless uniforms.

EAST JEFFERSON AVENUE AND BATES, 1894. This is a rare photograph of the Detroit Fire Department in action. Several different companies answered the alarm as the Edson Moore Dry Goods Company at 194 East Jefferson burns. There is an ambulance, several pump wagons, and a ladder wagon (foreground) desperately trying to contain the fire. Note the man at the top of the telephone pole in the middle of the photo.

WEST JEFFERSON AT CASS AVENUE, 1895. Another fire, this time involving the Dwyer and Vhay Fruit Market at 66 West Jefferson, occupies two steam pumpers as they battle a minor fire. The horses have been unhitched and led to safety. This is a good example of period equipment and uniforms.

JEFFERSON AVENUE AND RANDOLPH STREET, 1893. The fire department turns out on a cold January morning to fight a blaze at the high school. Unfortunately, they were unable to save the building. A wagon from number six company stands in front of the Detroit Electric Light and Power Company and Howard's Restaurant.

CASS AND HANCOCK AVENUES, 1895. Two years after the disastrous fire at the high school, the new Central High School opened its doors to students. Now known as "Old Main" and located on the campus of Wayne State University, it has been recently restored to its former glory.

JEFFERSON AVENUE AT GRISWOLD, 1898. In April, the governor of Michigan ordered the Michigan National Guard to mobilize at Island Lake to start movement to Tampa, Florida, and to the Spanish-American War. The state would provide four regiments of infantry, the 31st through the 35th. These companies are seen preparing to move to the rail station.

JEFFERSON AVENUE AND SHELBY STREET, 1898. These guardsmen prepare to move to the railroad station for movement south. The state would eventually send 4,104 officers and men south in response to the president's mobilization call. Two regiments, the 34th and 35th, would see active service in Cuba under General Shafter.

GRISWOLD AND FORT STREETS, 1898.
The Wayne County contingent made
their way in formation to the railhead.
Approximately 1,000 men from Detroit
and Wayne County would serve during
the years 1898 and 1899. Many more
of them would fall victim to disease
than to Spanish bullets. Some would die
in Florida.

USS MICHIGAN, 1898. This sailor, a
member of the armored cruiser *Michigan*,
is a typical example of the type of men
serving in the United States Navy during
this time. The Michigan Naval Reserves,
11 officers and 270 men, would serve
honorably on the USS *Yosemite*.
Several of these men were Detroiters,
such as Henry Joy, Edwin Denby, and
Truman Newberry.

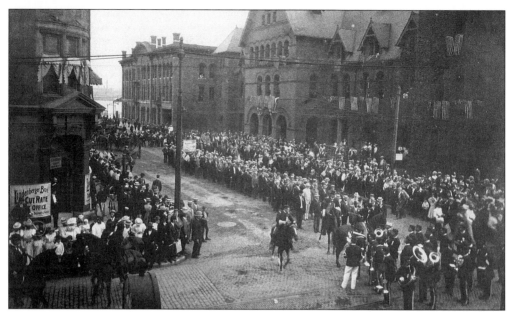

WOODBRIDGE AND THIRD STREETS, 1899. The band is playing and the crowd gathered to welcome home Detroiter Russell Alger, secretary of war under Presidents McKinley and Roosevelt. Alger had the difficult task of running the conflict logistically, a job for which he was heavily censored. Alger and his family lived at Fort and First Streets.

WOODWARD AVENUE AT CAMPUS MARTIUS, 1899. A huge crowd gathers in front of city hall to hear the welcoming speeches of various dignitaries to ex-Secretary of War Russell Alger. This photograph was taken on August 2, 1899, as the number of straw boaters will attest to the season.

WOODWARD AND MICHIGAN AVENUES, 1890S. This gentleman walks past the cannon on the city hall lawn. Long a Detroit landmark, these cannons were captured from the British after Commodore Perry's victory on Lake Erie during the War of 1812. Fred Sanders's ice cream parlor and Whitney's music store are in the familiar background.

MICHIGAN AVENUE, 1890S. A long view of the "other" avenue looking west from Abbott Street shows a wide variety of business establishments. The lady on the right side of the street is passing by the Palace Steam Laundry, the Sullivan & Buchanan furniture store, and a restaurant, while in the far distance can be seen the J.M. Flinn Ice Cream Company. Note the complete view of the light tower.

125

WOODWARD AVENUE AT CAMPUS MARTIUS, 1898. The venerable Russell House is seen in this view of a major Detroit intersection. All of the streetcars are powered by electricity, yet some citizens still travel by carriage. Detroit streets are still illuminated by overly tall light towers which fizzle and spark.

WOODWARD AVENUE BETWEEN GRATIOT AND WILCOX STREET, 1890s. Fred Sanders stands with two of his counter assistants in front of his new ice cream parlor and bakery at 180 Woodward. To the left is William Stoup's millinery shop, while to the right is the shop of Coulson and Marhous, who sold house furnishings.

CHILDREN'S PARADE, 1899. These children make up part of a parade, possibly a Labor Day affair. They are lined up on a side street, ready to begin, while a street vendor hawks his wares. Straw boaters, flags, and placards are plentiful.

WOODWARD AVENUE, 1899. A Labor Day parade proceeds down Woodward Avenue, past the Washington Market, as an overflowing crowd looks on. The Detroit Mounted Police keeps the crowd in check as a band moves by. Folks take advantage of empty wagon beds to obtain a better view of the proceedings.

WOODWARD AVENUE AT CAMPUS MARTIUS, 1890S. Winter has descended on the city, and the century, in this birds-eye view of the Campus Martius. J.L.Hudson is closing out his first big store and will move to the west side of Woodward. The new century will necessitate many changes in the character and complexion of the city. In a few short years this intersection will change completely as Detroit enjoys more growth and prosperity. Newer and bigger businesses will erect taller buildings as the downtown area progresses in the twentieth century. Gone are the trolleys and streetcars, the impossibly tall light towers, the opera house, and the city hall. To come is the automobile, and with it an unimaginable lifestyle and pace of life. Through it all, the Soldiers and Sailors Monument remains.